MAKING CONVERSATIONS COUNT

TRAINING PROGRAMME FOR

TEAMS & INDIVIDUALS

www.wagassociates.com 2020 ™

ISBN: 978-1-8382325-1-1

First published 2020

Dedication

To my Pop
The first man in my life that always
believed in me and all that I was
capable of…I know in my
heart you still believe

Contents

Preface

Who is this book for?

Making Conversations Count is for people who have a passion for their business that want to connect with new customers on a real human level.

What you will get?

My aim is to take you step by step through a focused and interactive approach.

How will we share this knowledge?

In part I will be sharing knowledge as well as taking you through some real exercises.

When can you start using our tips?

I hope that you can implement my tips immediately. As fast as you can read!

Please feel free to write in the margins, make notes where prompted and get in touch if you have a burning question at the end.

The Benefits of your Trainer

The benefits of the resources in this book come from my personal and professional experiences.

Experience – gained from 30+ years shared in corporate team environments

Resilience – has successfully traded through two recessions and a pandemic

Mastery – recruiter, interviewer, trainer, and mental health first aider

Convenience – learn at your own pace and return to relevant chapters

Value for money – get all that I teach for the cost of this book

Tailored – adapt the content to your business and specific needs

Flexible – adjust the content, delivery style and pace to suit you

Confidence – access a Facebook group to discuss matters in confidence

Team Building – work with others, share experiences and network

Fun – interactive, creative, and implementable

Acknowledgements

As a lover of language and a lover of books, it is an honour to write my first.

As someone who uses words daily to communicate, it is strange it took so long to get around to.

My hope is this book will help people embrace the phone in their business like I have.

Huge thanks to those I respect who planted the seed of an idea that I had this book in me. In particular:

The work wife, Colette Bratton of Marketing Angel, whom together we have delivered to hundreds of delegates in our Domino Effect workshops.

Jenny Proctor of Bondfield Marketing whom I have been delighted to guest on her podcast and work on client campaigns together.

And the first trainer I ever encountered on a six-week programme at 17 whose teachings have stayed with me, Pamela Belle-Ash, wherever you are now.

Introduction

Hello...This is your wake-up call!

How many of you have had to grow up at 7 years old? An early wake-up call.

I did not know then I showed extraordinary inner resilience at a tender age after my parents split up and I ran away from home. I was a Daddy's girl.

A chequered upbringing with truancy and custody battles before my 10th birthday. A strict stepfather in my teens terrified yet steadied me.

Thwarted by 2 years teacher training strikes in the mid 80's, I had to knuckle down to turn my life around to get the best grades I could, after missing such a lot of school. I grew a pair...

It was apparent to me I was the only person that could affect how I really wanted to live as a grown up.

At 13 years old, I bartered a job on the market working on the jeans and jacket stall. All heavy lifting! I beat the boy's time setting up and taking down the stall and won the job.

At 15, waitressing in the local pub gave a second income and at 16 was trained in silver service waitressing which made great tips.

By the time I was 17, I had 3 jobs. I was enjoying earning money, but home had become toxic again.

Spying an advert billed for strictly over 21-year olds I applied. I got the interview. I got the job. The weekend and evening work on my CV won me the interview.

My mature outlook in the interview, despite full of cold, won me the job.

The moral early on was clear to strive for a better life and break the mould. My Uncle says I could have headed for jail…no, sir!

Dealing with people has been the key ingredient to every job I had. It has followed me time and again throughout my career with a no stopping me attitude.

Couple that with getting a huge kick out of helping people.

Sales was my mask so to speak. The phone my protector. I was whomever I wanted to be. It was my escape. How about you?

I have a natural lean to recruiting, training, and project managing outbound teams.

When I reached 30, I had repetitive laryngitis and had to have my tonsils removed. Losing my voice nearly lost me everything.

I was not speaking my truth. This insight is now my gift to share with you. **Speak your truth in all that you do.**

So, since 2005, I have been helping my clients by delivering telemarketing campaigns, training and delivering sales & marketing workshops.

Satisfaction comes from being able to share my knowledge and see it work. Even my eldest is in marketing now!

My tips could be the difference you have been searching for, so your business performs better.

Are you ready for your wake-up call?!

Hello!!!

I am Wendy and I would really like to talk to you about "Making Conversations Count".

Foreword

Jane Pallister, M.Sc.

MD Boommm Consultancy & Training and Entrepreneur in Residence, Staffordshire University

In my media sales career and since starting my business twenty years ago, the importance of getting to the right people and creating instant appeal and engagement has always been uppermost.

I have advised thousands of businesses in my consultancy and advisory career, and worked with giants like eBay on their business trader start-up course.

Wendy and I met through our respective businesses, and we struck an instant note with each other and formed a solid professional friendship. As someone who is a published academic, I rate people who take time to hone their craft, are customer focussed, and work tirelessly to become best in field.

Wendy is one of those rare people who talks sense, oozes practicality, and gets to the nub of a communications problem really quickly.

Her experience, successes and insights are impressive and immediately actionable.

Wendy has impressed hundreds of clients since she started her business.

This is one book which will take you to where you need to be in terms of making those first connections. Especially in these strange times, where making the right approach is critical.

Read. Learn. Apply. Succeed.

Find Jane here: www.boommm.com

How will we work together through this book?

Let me put it this way and make a start:

How much new business do you want?

Think £££'s – is it per client or per box shifted?

Where will you find these people?

Who are you already doing business with that you could find more of the same?

What are you going to say to get their attention?

Four questions that seem blindingly obvious, but where we need to make a start.

Q: Why? The hardest lesson is knowing your money.

Either way you could be selling a time based service or boxed goods – you will need to know how much of your time needs to be booked or how many boxes you need to sell to reach your financial target.

For example, if you need to earn an extra £1000 a month, it will break down into a certain number of new customers.

If you have 100 boxes that will make you £10 each you have your £1000. You will need to 'sell' to 100 people unless you are offering a deal to encourage buying more than one.

If you have a service led package you will need to work out how much time it takes to deliver and how many you can comfortably fit into a week. You may need fewer people to sell to but the road to commitment may well be longer.

Larger companies need to factor in their overheads and all sorts of complicated numbers.

Already you should have an idea of how many.

Answer it here:

Then, follow what gives you joy and brings out a natural passion that is hard to turn off. That fire in your belly will be what wins the day for you.

Whether you are a solopreneur or the boss of a multimillion-pound operation you need to know your numbers first before you start talking to anyone.

Next comes finding the right people.

Q: Where do they hang out?

You need to think about a marriage between the following two factors to get your winning formula.

Q: Who do you work with already that you love working with?

The one that is a dream to work with or the most fun to work with. Then think about the customer that you make the most money from.

Mix the two together and you will see a pattern forming in your top three clients.

Now you have a selection process to find the right companies and the right people at those companies. Remember you already have a great track record in dealing with these types of client and you will be working to your true values.

And of course, now you know how many people you need to be talking to. Manageable and does not seem that bad, does it?!

If you are just starting out, I would draw on your past experiences and highlight the strengths you bring with you to your new venture.

Making sense so far? Good...

Because now you need to get their attention and "Make Conversation Count"

My approach to conversation is it does not matter whether it is an online or offline interaction.

There is no getting away from the digital age.

Social media plays a massive role in influencing us in our private lives.

Well, it is no different for businesses through mediums where they can advertise, and people can find what they are looking for.

Since people make up the running of businesses too, it is often where we will begin talking to them through our content messages.

You need to be sharing as much information as you can in your online conversations to persuade these people, they must only explore their needs with you.

This will attract inbound leads and are the best kind.

However, my own opinion is that as a small business owner it can be a relentless task to keep the online conversation going.

We must create conversations in the real world.

It is by building relationships with people and offering the right solution that forms the winning combination.

I hope to share ways of doing this through the book and in further chapters we will cover topics such as:

- How to plan and write a winning script
- How to handle and get past gatekeepers
- How to handle objections and turn them into positive buying signals
- How to structure a telemarketing campaign
- How to cope with 'rejection' and gain/maintain motivation
- How to build confidence on the phone and use it to your advantage
- How and when to ask for the opportunity to do business
- How to make the appointment, the next steps and follow up effectively
- How to effectively nurture a pipeline of opportunities and generate sales
- How to create a Client for Life programme

I will try to turn the sales jargon into real world language and demystify it.

If you do not see a chapter titled one of these how to do, don't worry it will all be covered.

Common sense is the key ingredient. Plus knowing your onions.

We are dealing with people.

Who, let's face it, are a sociable bunch who buy from people like themselves, right?

The benefits of working through this book together, will be:

Audit your sales and marketing processes reinforcing your Customer Value Proposition or CVP.

Basically, Cost Volume Profit makes more sense to me.

Q: What does it cost; how many do I need to sell and at what price to make a profit?

But some smart Alec came up with a fancier term that puts the customer at the forefront of the proposal.

Hidden behind all of that is the promise you make the client. The quality of the product or service. The why Mr Customer should use you and not Mr Competition.

This is just one level up from my first question to you, about knowing your numbers. Plus:

Q: Why buy from you?

Answer it here:

Do not worry, this may change but it is good to have a starting point.

Identify improvement

Sales & marketing has been around for a very long time. The tools used come in and out of fashion. To my mind marketing should come before sales.

Social selling should be combined with Solution selling.

Having lots of tools at your disposal does not necessarily mean they are all the right ones to be concentrating on. You need to identify a proven method of engagement for your business.

Only concentrate on the mediums that work.

Any others should be watched, tested, and measured over time to prove worthwhile of your time, activity, and investment.

Q: What are your top three platforms for online sales?

Answer it here:

Q: What new tool would you like to try?

Answer it here:

Do you have quiet times?

Being able to plan, prepare and position around your seasonal calendar will allow you to market for the quiet times.

When you identify these times, you can begin to plan your activity around the buying cycle.

Think about it.

Create an offer to encourage purchases in your usual quiet times.

This will bring you less of a dip and leverage more revenue.

Example: Christmas can be the peak of business yet January dips dramatically. Hence, we have the January Sales.

Q: When are your quiet times?

Answer it here:

Q: What can you offer to improve sales over the quiet time?

Answer it here:

Who's on your team?

Freelancers, external consultants, and/or paid staff are all customer facing, dealing with different situations.

Each partner department needs to represent the whole business and communicate with each other on behalf of your customers.

Creating company values and aligning them with everyone involved in your business forges a focused team.

By going the extra mile internally your team will create the best customer experience.

Q: What core value is most important to you?

Answer it here:

Who is responsible?

Assign clear guidance and support of who needs to action what tasks. This will inevitably sharpen the whole teams focus and performance.

Customers notice this stuff!

Do you need database management to draw down specific selections?

There are so many options for customer relationship management software platforms on the market. So, this will come down to scale.

A simple excel spreadsheet can do the same job if you are working with a few hundred names. But whilst writing this book, I have moved to Hubspot which is free. There are paid for addons but if you're just starting out free will do fine.

Q: How many contact records will you need to manage?

Answer it here:

Q: How do you plan to communicate aside from the telephone contact?

Answer it here:

Consider your database as the platform for your business to identify the following:

- Safely store and centralise your contacts and activities.
- Plan your daily tasks.
- Activity reports.
- Targeting data segments.
- Email integration for mass messaging.
- Track your success.

It will fast become the brains of your operation!

Research and target new audiences

Google is a great tool for research yet...LinkedIn is the go-to platform for exploring people and industries all in one place.

Think back to the question I asked you earlier. What is the perfect marriage of clients you work for now? Who do you want to replicate?

Q: What industries do they work in?

Answer it here:

Q: Have you identified a new marketplace?

Answer it here:

Q: Where do you want to geographically work?

Answer it here:

The Covid-19 pandemic has meant businesses have found new ways to serve customers. It is still my opinion, to serve our local community first offers the best foundation.

Be the big fish in your local pond.

Generate appointments, qualified leads, and pipelines

Embracing a sales process will enable your business to grow. Understanding who you want to speak to makes finding them simpler. All because you know what they want to talk about.

Q: What solution do they want and don't have?

Answer it here:

Q: What problem do they have you can fix?

Answer it here:

Q: Write a list of 10 new companies to work with.

Answer it here:

Realistically it would be great if the way I show you becomes a habit that makes your life much simpler and easier to sell more!

The bones of your sales process

Database

- Understand why you capture data.
- Be confident knowing your way around.
- Store the important information.

Q: What data is important to capture?

Answer it here:

Products

- Know your products.
- Know how your products solve problems.
- Create a Frequently asked questions guide.

Q: What are the benefits to customers?

Answer it here:

Case Studies

- Create crib sheets for easy reference.
- Match products to customers in case studies.
- Use customers to attract similar customers.
- Share customers stories in the same industry sectors.

Q: Who have you worked for and how did it help them?

Answer it here:

Marketing

- Use email templates to save time.
- Create pdf brochures to support your message.
- Point customers to info on your website.
- Create social media content.

Q: What other marketing can you create?

Answer it here:

Script

- ❖ Bullet point the vital details you want to capture.
- ❖ Qualify with questions to get them talking.
- ❖ Identify opportunities by listening.
- ❖ Relay real life scenarios with story telling.

Q: What approach will you take to encourage the conversation?

Answer it here:

Campaign

- ❖ What do you want the customers to take away from your contact with them?

Q: What will you be promoting as a product or service?

Answer it here:

Set realistic goals. What makes it a success through making contact?

Think about it…

By making contact with the right people in the right places you should see:

- Your website traffic increase.
- Your followers on social media increase.
- Your brand awareness increase.

Q: What else should increase?

Answer it here:

Plan where your activity will be anchored.

Q: Will it be in a certain industry?

Answer it here:

Q: Will it be in a certain location?

Answer it here:

You can try a few different ideas at the same time. But that is not for the faint hearted. You need to be able to test and measure. If it runs away with you – scale it back.

Targets

Desired outcomes from the campaign should be thought out and measured. Have an idea of your goals. It will help you set and reach targets to show your success.

Example:

From a list of 10 companies you should be able to complete the following tasks:

- Identify the right person.
- Speak to that person.
- Email them more information.
- Qualify their need for your services.
- Agree the next action.
- Invite them to join your network.

You may not reach all ten. You may not complete every task. Especially the speak to them. But it will be a good indicator for you to measure the potential of converting them to a customer.

There is potential here to be very specific and repeat the activity in different industries and locations.

Generating sales will be the key driver however be realistic in finding someone who is read to buy on that first call.

Following making contact you must qualify their potential need. It means you will be creating a future pipeline of people to follow up in your diary.

You can mark these in different ways to show where they are in the process. For example, I use KIT as a task phrase. It means Keep In Touch. I have spoken to them and we have agreed to speak again at a specific time. It is really helpful when you have a long list of people on your list. Those with KIT automatically become the priority calls. It is important to do what is promised and follow up. By understanding where they are, what priorities they have, you stay in the game and build trust.

Those you were unable to reach by telephone should be added to a constant contact list. The constant contact tactic is to not let 90 days go by before you try again.

There are many reasons why a person will not take a sales call.

In the main, it is usually about timing.

By sending appropriate email correspondence you can begin to build the relationship. Your brand is being displayed and will encourage engagement later.

The context of the email will be a soft introduction. It should state the problem or solution you help most people with. It should also give them an expectation of what you will do next. The focus is not on getting them to respond. They are busy with other things. My emails tend to sign off with something like:

"I'm guessing you are busy with other things right now so I will try again in [days or weeks' time] unless I hear otherwise from you."

This is clear that you appreciate their time. This is clear you will try again. This is clear they can help you out by responding. The response can be:

- Happy for now – you judge when the next best time will be to try again. Relationships change. The solution can change. Reply saying you will keep in touch and thank them.
- Let's look at this [they give a specific time] – They have given you a timescale. Reply and say thank you. Let them know you appreciate the opportunity and look forward to that time.
- No reply – this is a constant contact call

Q: What is a realistic target for you to set?

You may want to break the target down into smaller goals. For example, for every ten people you have on your list:

- Call everyone = 10
- Email everyone = 10
- Connect with everyone = 5
- Speak to everyone = 2
- Qualify everyone = 2

When I worked in logistics, we had two simple targets. It was proven that if we hit the first target, the second target became easier. It was to send out 10 brochures per day. So, 50 brochures a week. This would have a domino effect on the appointments generated through follow up calls. Our target was two appointments a day. Meaning 10 appointments a week. Giving us a one in five conversion. It equates to emails sent personally too. And, follows the targets I've loosely outlined above.

You give it a try and track it. Let me know how it works for you.

Answer it here:

Competitor Research

I've asked you lots of questions about your business, your offering, who you want to speak to and why. But here is a biggie...

Q: Who is your competition?

Now I am not asking you all this to point out how great your competition is. It is important to check this stuff on a quarterly or half yearly basis. Your competition is unlikely to stand still.

New ideas create waves in the market, and it is up to you to be able to spot any potential tsunami that could affect your business.

It should give you great confidence to talk about your business! When you know what you are up against, it is much easier to stay focused on your why.

Answer it here:

Name three:

Q: What are they doing better than you?

Answer it here:

Q: What are they doing that is worse than you?

Answer it here:

Q: How did you do on the comparison?

Answer it here:

Q: Who would you buy from?

Answer it here:

The Important Questions

This list of questions will not change but your answers may later...

Let's answer the following questions and come back to them. As we work through the chapters you can compare later.

- Why should businesses use the telephone?

- Develop a campaign agenda – what is the reason for your call?

- What are the key objectives from the call?

- How will you break the data into segments for best targeting?

- How will you research your prospects?

- Outline the loose 'script' you will use?

- When will calling fit within your role? E.g. number hours/days etc

- Do you need an ice breaker or hook?

- What may be a good action to agree at the end of the call?

- What will you send them to support your call?

- Are you geared up for incoming calls?

- Where will you record the intelligent information from the calls?

- How will you measure your success?

- How will you deal with customers saying no?

Let's get down to answering these questions.

The one big benefit of using the phone to connect with customers must be the transference of passion in our voice.

We make a judgement almost instantly whether we are prepared to give someone our ears to listen to what they have to offer.

No-one wants to be 'sold' to so your approach to opening the conversation is THE most important step.

Creating that best 1st impression will be the foundation to building the relationship with the customer and determine the journey you wish to take them on with you.

Please do not put on a posh accent or try to sound like Mrs Bouquet!

Think about it. Be yourself.

There are three types of tone:

- Non-assertive.
- Aggressive.
- Assertive.

You can imagine how they sound, right?

Now it can get really technical when you delve into the tone of voice. I want to make it as simple as I can. I am not qualified as a voice coach. However, I have a trained ear, from over 30 years of wearing a headset, and honing my listening skills!

The first tip

Is to match the speed the other person is speaking.

If they are excited, they will speak quickly.

If they are explaining, they will speak slower.

The second tip

Is to understand the four personality types in sales:

The Driver – this personality type is assertive. They get to the point, have a plan, and stand out.

The Amiable – this personality values honesty. They build trust and rapport.

The Analytical – focuses on the numbers, they prepare, research, and decide on facts.

The Expressive – can be impulsive, energetic, and open. They appreciate case studies and storytelling.

Not everyone fits perfectly into one category, but it may help you to think about your own style of communicating. That will be more comfortable when tackling sales.

The third tip

Is to understand the four types of customers and their buying personas:

Price buyers – lowest price drives the decision. They have little interest in value, differentiation, or relationships.

Relationship buyers – trust and dependable relationships with suppliers drives their decision. They need to know they will be taken care of.

Value buyers – looking to create value in the relationship. They are wanting additional efficiencies, reduced costs, increased sales, or margins.

Poker Player buyers – sneaky relationship or value buyers disguised as price buyers to gain the best deal for the lowest price.

Depending on where you look these types will go by other names, but it gives you a feel and flavour of how to identify the best tactic for a deal to transact successfully.

Think about it.

It can even help you identify the types of people you do not want to do business with! Whilst you may have an ideal customer in mind at what cost will you take them? If they are rude? They will likely be a royal pain. If they only value price? How low will you go for the time and effort? Kudos brand names can be a drain on your time for little profit. Please do not fall into a trap purely for the turnover it brings. Move on. There are lots of fish in your pond…

We have already talked about identifying the most ideal customer to work with. Now you need to do some research. Find them and create a list ready for contacting them.

Google maps will find companies listing a business page. Links to their website and phone number. Look at their website to judge a good fit. Are there social icons to take you through to LinkedIn etc.? Find the right person in the business. Take a copy of their profile link and save it in your database.

Let us start with 10 people:

1.

2.

3.

4.

5.

6.

7.

8.

9.

10.

Next is your purpose.

Q: What is the reason you want to contact them?

And I do not mean so you can ask them to buy from you!

I mean you need to identify what solution you have and why you will be the best person to fix it for them.

Think about THEIR agenda.

This opportunity is to establish how they do things now. Who are they using? What plans have they in the future? When will it be a priority? Are they a prospect?

Answer it here:

Please do not expect someone to be prime and ready to purchase from you on your first call!

This is just the first step for you to introduce yourself. Manage expectations – both your own and the customers. Expect to be asked to send more information. Yes, it is a fob off but it is also a test. Will you send it? Will you follow up? YES!

Q: What will you send them?

Answer it here:

Brochures, Case Studies, Video Testimonials are all great mediums to show Proof. Let the customer see how you have helped already. Your existing customers saying great things about you is far better than you blowing your own trumpet.

The hard salespeople will push the customer.

"What information do you need that I cannot answer now for you?"

Now think how that makes you feel?

Yeah, turned off after making a great start, right?

Do not make the mistakes of the stereotypical salesperson.

Your success will be to ask them:

"Is there anything specific you need covered in the information and I will make sure it is included."

This will depend on where they are in the buying cycle. They may prioritise a case study over a technical brochure? You can send them both.

By continuing to ask smart questions you will strengthen their initial judgement. It will help you build the rapport to be invited to stay in contact.

The customer will expect you to lead with what the next action will be and gives you control of the conversation.

You have options depending on what you have discussed:

- If it is time that is limited. Send information to introduce yourself, email it to give them chance to look over the details.
- It could be that the customer is not ready to begin the buying journey. Be sure to ask when what you are offering will become a priority.

That will allow you to define when the next best time will be to be in touch. It also becomes an agreed action.

EXAMPLE:

When a product has a long shelf life, like a computer or copier, it will be replaced approximately every 3 – 5 years.

Asking the age of their current equipment can lead to an obvious statement. There is unlikely to be a need if it only 6 months old. Or that there could be a need if it is 4 years old.

One tactic that will prove to be important in most cases will be TIMING.

It will be refreshing for a customer to hear someone say "I don't want to be taking up your time if it is not a priority yet."

The relief for the customer to say no, not yet is usually palpable.

Therefore, using the example of age of their equipment allows you to easily identify their place in the buying cycle without needing to throw your whole sales pitch at them.

This approach allows you to build the relationship.

Ask when you can be invited to follow up and keep your promise to call when agreed.

It is a good idea to send an email thanking them for their time. Outline how you can help when the time is right. Explain when you will get back to them.

Offer yourself as approachable in the meantime as it is appreciated by all buyers.

I tend to sign off with a note saying should they have any questions in the meantime I am happy to answer them.

Attach those pdf documents you have created in your arsenal, particularly those that explain how you have helped a customer in a similar circumstance.

Your objective is to qualify they will be in the market for what you do. Then establish when that is going to be.

This will build your pipeline and grow your prospect list. When you build a list of potential customers, it is important to concentrate on one sector at a time.

Stick with one message at a time.

This way you will be able to measure the success of each campaign and message. Allowing you to review and concentrate on where you are most successful.

Test and measure.

It is possible to use the internet and social media to research the people in the business.

Often, companies have a 'Meet The Team' page explaining who does what.

Sometimes they add contact details like mobile numbers and email addresses too.

LinkedIn is a fantastic resource to easily research the right person.

This can be helpful in identifying who you want to speak to and gives confidence when ringing and asking for that person.

However, there is a caveat to LinkedIn that it can be like Wikipedia. It is only as accurate as the humans keeping it up to date.

You will find enhancing your LinkedIn profile a good exercise. It will then clearly state what you do and who for. A good springboard to invite your target customers to connect.

You may well find other interests from reading their profile that you share. These can be a good hook to begin the conversation.

You can use this within your invitation message.

Once they accept the invitation you can decide how you wish to start the conversation. Will it be in the messaging or by picking up the phone to thank them for the connection?

Picking up the phone is my preference however I do use messaging too. It is the perfect time to start a chat.

I use the analogy of the biggest networking room on the planet.

It is as though we have just met at a networking event.

When you message (or phone!) it is a good idea to use icebreakers or conversation starters.

By saying “Thank you for connecting” and adding:

Monday message: How was your weekend?

Tuesday message: Have you got a busy week?

Wednesday message: Do you recommend any networking events?

Thursday message: Are you having a busy week?

Friday message: Have you got plans this weekend?

None of these messages are directly about work or what they do or what you offer.

It is about getting to know them a little better. It gives you some insight as to whether they will reciprocate with a question.

You get to gauge how conversational they are. How open are they to moving the relationship on?

There will be some who do not respond at all, that is fine.

There will be some that just answer the question.

There will be some that answer and ask you questions.

The best ones will respond to your question, ask you more and begin a flow of deeper questions about what you do.

These are the ones that are prime to move to a conversation in the real world.

Now I am cheering!

How you do that will be based on how comfortable you are in asking.

You might simply ask if they are open for a quick call there and then since you are messaging.

You may want to say you would welcome exploring more. Do they have a diary link?

You may have a diary link you can share with them. This leaves you waiting for them to act. Be sure it is followed up.

But how good would it be if you could turn LinkedIn into a prospect generating machine?

Filling up your diary with a few simple steps.

For those that don't accept your invitation, or converse on LinkedIn, or those that you cannot find, you will need to pick up the phone.

Q: What will you say to them?

Answer it here:

Q: What will your loose script be?

Answer it here:

People I have worked with on a 121 basis through my Power Up sessions have learned how to use LinkedIn. They benefit from an intuitive and creative thought process that applies to them.

It is often ourselves that is in our own way of picking up the phone. Too many procrastinating reasons why they won't want to speak to us or that we will be interrupting.

The simple truth is you are looking to introduce yourself. You do not need to go into a full-blown script from the off.

Here is my take on it and there's more on LinkedIn later:

I am not an advocate of scripted calls.

We can all tell when we receive one, can't we?

The person calling tends to not be very good at listening. They don't know what to do if you ask them something that is not the next step on the script. You should not have these challenges when:

- You know your product or service inside out.
- You know every detail.
- You know what objections they will have.
- You know what questions a new customer asks.
- You know how you can solve their problem.

The most important person on the first and every call is the customer.

The best questions you can ask are all about where they are now and what their plans are around it.

Okay, so now you have a semblance of a plan.

Go back to the beginning. Think about how many customers you will need and break it down to per month, per week and per day.

You had a list of ten.

Q: How many lists of ten do you need to contact per month?

Answer it here:

Here are some statistics that will help you work out how much time you need to dedicate to finding and converting new customers per month.

These figures will be relative to a 3 – 6 month period of activity.

200 new people identified

100 new people reached

40 new people qualified with potential

8 buyer ready

These figures are a good average for measuring your £££'s and time.

This works out as making 10 phone calls per day which ought to take a little over an hour. 20 calling days per month.

Eight new customers might be too many or not enough but what this does illustrate is that it is very manageable and doable.

Ready to get on the phone now?!!

Great news!

Just a few more things before you do!

You know who you want to speak to, but you need to keep a track. Remember we covered databases? The simplest way is an excel spreadsheet or Hubspot to get fancy and free. Think about the relevant information and if it's searchable.

Consider what data is important to you that will help you get closer to the customer buying from you.

We look, later in the book, at the types of data that is intelligent. Which you can adapt to your needs. This information can be drawn upon for specific purposes at a given time. For example, if you want to send a special offer to specific groups of prospects. You need to have identified them in a group and have their contact details, such as email address to send it to.

Above all, you need to capture when the next contact will take place and record it!

You never want to miss a call back!

This will become your pipeline of potential customers. You have worked hard to identify them. You have agreed to contact them when the time is right.

Keep notes on all that you spoke about and the actions you took. I tend to enter the date and notes into the same text box so that it reads with the latest note first, when I work in Excel.

Plus, three columns that can track how long it has taken to complete the buying cycle. For example, the first contact date, last contact date and next contact date.

Data sorting the next contact date will list your activities and give you a working call calendar.

Software based CRM systems automatically time stamp entries for you to see how long it took to convert a customer.

Those eight potential customers may span months or years depending on the buying cycle in your business.

It is important to keep filing the pipeline up because you will be able to forecast potentially busy periods too.

Over a measurable, period of time you will begin to measure your successes as you convert prospects to customers.

Be sure to maintain the activity or risk a dip in business revenue. Even when you are really busy it's crucial to maintain new business activity.

One final pointer.

Remember: there are more customers than you can ever serve...And, not every customer will be willing to consider a different supplier.

Not every customer is worth serving!

Your focus needs to be on those that say they are interested even if it is not yet.

It is okay for a customer to say no. You have many more potential customers you can serve.

We never win them all!

HOWEVER

My own clients have said great things about the approach I encourage.

Everyone has their own unique personality and way of doing things, yet it is the process that works.

By following this method, my customers have seen a revenue growth between 12-18% which is impressive!

Check out my profile for the many recommendations I have received. There is a blend for either:

Helping on LinkedIn

Using the telephone

Or Both 😊

https://www.linkedin.com/in/wendyannharris

Best Practices

Jumping on the phone is governed by regulation to protect everyone.

This chapter gives you an overview of this regulation. Where you can find support ensuring that you comply and stay up to date.

Data + GDPR + CTPS

This is an important combination and are the key to gain success – both for direct mail and telemarketing campaigns.

It is imperative that your data is cleaned regularly – every 6 months you can expect 40% of your records to have some change, whether it be a decision maker contact change, an address change, a CTPS registration etc.

Data cleaning should be inexpensive; with regular contact to customers and prospects your information should remain as up to date as possible.

100% clean is a misconception due to lots of movement in any market.

When you start out, it is a good idea to make sure the companies you want to contact are open to receiving telephone marketing calls.

The Corporate Telephone Preference Service or CTPS for short. It is a database where companies can register against contact from businesses they have never had any dealings with.

You can find out more via the website https://www.tpsonline.org.uk/tps/whatiscorporatetps.html

GDPR legislation was introduced in May 2018 to reinforce the Data Protection Act. It will be relevant to your company policy and will affect the way you process data.

All companies storing data are by law expected to be registered with the Information Commissioners Office (ICO) and have a policy in place relating to how staff manage data.

The ICO website is a useful resource https://ico.org.uk/

Please refer to this and feel free to contact them as they are very helpful in ensuring your company's policies are watertight.

Phew! It's good to keep this bit to two pages and get you to bring in the experts on it.

I know a few so get in touch if you struggle...

Intellectual Data Gathering

Telemarketing is not just about booking appointments or generating leads and sales, it is also about gathering intellectual data.

This allows you to build profiles on your prospects and forecast future sales.

Ensure when you are gathering intellectual data that you record it.

An example of intellectual data could be:

- What industry is the prospect in?
- Has there been any history with the prospect?
- Current Suppliers?
- Turnover per month?
- How many staff do they employ?
- Who do they use on a 1st, 2nd, 3rd basis?
- What are the reasons for their choices?
- When is their next review planned?
- Where did they go on holiday?
- How many children do they have?
- Have they finished that big project?

Your intelligence does not have to be all about work.

The best conversations are personal.

Communication

Clear communication throughout the campaign is very important. Think about your expectations for the campaign. Set yourself clear key performance indicators (KPI's). That way you can monitor throughout. You will not want be disappointed as you want the campaign to deliver the desired expectations.

Prepare for the call

Get ready for your calling sessions.

If you are new to making calls and are nervous, please do not worry.

This is a great sign that you care about the impression you are going to make and that you take it personally.

Those butterflies that you may feel in your tummy will get quieter, I promise.

Confidence will build and your conversations will grow.

This is the first step to many fantastic relationships you are going to build by being yourself over the phone.

All you need to do is prepare properly.

Always keep a glass of water on your desk.

The last thing you want is to suddenly have a tickle in your throat that leads to a coughing fit.

The more calls you do, the more knowledge you gain, the more leads you generate.

This increases your confidence and your profitability.

Prepare yourself before you hit your phone task list for the day.

Being sure you have full focus, concentration and purpose will be a big factor to achieving great results.

Give yourself the time and respect the task of calling deserves by ensuring distractions are out of mind.

My top tips to plan and prepare are:

1. Water – all that talking is thirsty work!
2. Stationary – pens, scrap paper – your brief and list of objections so you know what you are going to say.
3. Sufficient leads – the chances are high that you will make a lot of calls before you reach a decision maker to speak to.
4. Update your calendar with when to call them back so you do not miss any important calls!
5. Product knowledge – technical or specification sheets to remind you of the key features, advantages, and benefits. There is always one who asks an awkward question…

6. Do not disturb sign – be sure you block out enough time with no distractions. Be sure you have had a bathroom break and you are on out of office / busy on email.

7. Targets – be realistic about what you need to achieve in terms of outcomes required. If 10 calls are your target note how many people you spoke to and what the next actions look like.

8. And finally, a treat – when you reach target or agree a deal or book an appointment reward yourself. You have worked hard for it.

These tips will keep you focused, avoid disruption, and help you achieve targets.

Believe me when I say it works!

Brief

Prepare a clear brief. Similar to a script but the backbone of your campaign.

What is your campaign about?

- How is the campaign structured?
- How much clean data do you have?
- What intellectual data do you want to collate?
- What counts as the criteria for a "good" appointment / lead / sale?
- What is the Decision Maker Contact level?
- What are you hoping to achieve?
- What will the common objections be?
- How will you measure success?
- How will you deal with information requests?
- When will you manage the campaign day to day?

Quality Control

A good quality control procedure should be in place.

If an email address is typed incorrectly the email will not be delivered.

If a Decision Maker Contact name is spelt incorrectly it can reflect badly.

All company details should follow the same format. For example: Limited or Ltd not both.

Companies House is the best source for how the business has registered their name.

Here is the link:
https://beta.companieshouse.gov.uk/search/

Test & Measure

My experience is that any new campaign will glean feedback after a week.

Even with the best planning it is not always going to go as you first think.

You will need to monitor your activity and tweak where there are obvious ways to reset desired achievement levels.

It is not realistic to do so before the campaign is tested.

This may seem boring but if I do not tell you about it there's room for failing.

And I do not want that for you!

The reasons for this are:

Until the data is called you will not know its quality.

Every client's criteria for a sale/appointment/lead are different.

For example, if the brief is –

(i) Only book appointments with prospects doing over a set level of business OR

(ii) Only book appointments with Financial Directors OR

(iii) Look to handle prospects without a face to face meeting when under a qualified level of business

After the first week, you will have the knowledge to confirm future expectations.

Even after 30 years I am still surprised.

The variables will depend on your criteria and targets will be identified as you "farm" the data.

Allowing prospects to be profiled, means your opportunities will increase.

An example could be to set weekly targets.

1. the number of appointments or quotes

2. the number of information emails or letters

By doing this means you will know you are creating brand awareness in sending out marketing information.

You are positioning yourself in the customers mind's eye for potential buying opportunities.

Sharing your current customers experiences with new people builds trust.

You know you are visible, adding credibility for when you have the perfect opportunity to turn it into profitability.

LinkedIn

The biggest networking room on the planet.

First let us look at your positioning.

In a B2B marketplace, most people will be drawn to LinkedIn.

How many of us already use LinkedIn?

Millions of us!

Here are some tips on how to proposition your target audience and prepare them for what you want from them.

I have used this process as part of my telephone campaigns for many years and can vouch for its success for my clients and myself.

Great customer relationships come from managing expectations.

Your LinkedIn profile is the best snapshot any potential customer will get into who you are, how you help and why you love what you do.

This is where your relationship starts.

You need to present yourself in the best possible light.

Consider this your ‘personal splash page’ where people can find out everything about you that you wish them to know.

I am going to work through your profile page top to bottom and you may want to grab your phone or laptop to check these tips out as we go along.

Change your LinkedIn URL to your name.

You will find the edit your profile name in grey at the right-hand side of your profile page.

Common names are likely to be taken so a good idea can be to get creative.

If you are known as the Queen of or the King of or The XYZ Guru use that.

This name will follow you around so you could add your company name.

For example: I could use WendyHarrisWAG or QueenOfMakingConversationCount

Mine is: WendyAnnHarris but used to be WendyAnnGillett and where WAG comes from.

It is true that there is always a story behind every name – share it in a post!

Whatever you choose you can use it as a public URL. Use it to promote yourself and share it on email footers or business cards – to showcase you.

Be sure to add other URLs such as your Website, Blog or Twitter URL into the Contact Details section.

Word of caution though.

Please do not add any text other than your name in your Name section.

You risk your profile breaking LinkedIn's policy.

If you are a Guru or Queen of put this in the Headline section. Same with Emojis.

Optimise your Headline to say more than just your job title to get you noticed for how you can help.

Your headline is the second thing people will notice after your profile image and banner.

Make sure they can easily digest exactly who you help and why they should connect with you.

It is a great way to challenge yourself to summing up your offer in a sentence.

Use a professional looking photo of you.

Create a banner to advertise in images what you offer.

Utilise the Providing Services function.

LinkedIn use this to aid their search engine and push the most relevant matching profiles to those searching.

The About section should be about you.

Not the business – yet.

This is your opportunity to speak in the first person to all those customers that you are encouraging to read your profile.

Tell your story.

The first two lines of your about are visible before anyone must click see more.

Use this sentence as your hook.

It should be compelling.

Make them want to click see more.

They will be deciding whether they connect with you from what you write here.

I would also recommend looking at your account settings to change the right-hand side of your profile where it says, 'viewers of this profile also viewed'.

Turn this off.

You do not want to encourage them to go check out your competition. LinkedIn will be pushing profiles like yours otherwise.

You will find it under profile information in your account settings.

Whilst you are there take note of some of the other settings too.

You may not want anyone seeing your connections...

Featured posts are the best way to showcase the information you need your customers to see.

Perfect for adding your brochure, your video and client case studies in one easy to access area.

Treat this like your VIP section.

You can scroll across these posts and make the best three prominent.

Your Dashboard keeps a track of your activity.

It is always worth taking a screenshot of these figures so you can monitor improvement.

How many people have viewed your profile in the last 90 days?

Most recent post views.

How many search appearances in the last week?

Click on the blue numbers for more details on who has viewed your profile, where they work and what they do.

By completing your profile with relevant 'Keywords' that describe how you help you will attract the right people to view your profile.

It also raises your profile to appear as high as possible on Google and LinkedIn searches.

Keep your profile as full as possible too – LinkedIn provide you with a gauge of 'completeness'.

Strive to be 100% complete or All Star.

The Experience section is where you talk in the third person about the businesses you work for and have worked at.

My view is that three or four roles are plenty unless the amount of time is less than 10 years.

People are generally only interested in what you are doing well now.

Add media marketing documents to your roles.

Seeing the corporate brochure or video here adds weight to your branding story.

Complete your Education and Voluntary section.

Skills & Endorsements are often overlooked however they are a great way to add kudos to you.

These skills are now in your control.

You can add, edit and rearrange them too. I've added chatterbox for some fun!

They are also searchable adding to your credibility when someone is looking for what you do.

A great way to show your support, to someone you know that maybe you have not worked with but would like to, is to endorse them at skills you admire in them.

Remember me saying that your Headline will be the second thing people notice after your Profile and Banner image?

Recommendations are the third.

Think about it.

Recommendations mean you are vouched for by someone else.

You have no control over what they say.

What they say will resonate with the reader looking to engage with what you do.

This acts like a referral would.

You are credible.

You are worth having a conversation with.

A great way to gain recommendations is to give them.

Think about people you have worked with and make a list of at least five.

Write them a recommendation and send it to them from their profile.

What you are doing here will a. be a pleasant surprise and b. trigger them to reciprocate.

Accomplishments covers all the areas you may struggle to add information into your profile in other areas.

Publications you have produced or featured in, patents you have on products, courses or projects completed, honours and awards, test scores etc.

Think about it.

Have you taken a course since leaving education that awarded you a certificate?

Have you featured an article in a magazine?

Perhaps you have been a guest on a podcast? Add this to Publications and help promote the channel.

Add your Interests.

Focus on what your customers will feel is important to them.

There are many ways to enhance your profile.

Do not neglect it.

Your best conversations are likely to start on LinkedIn – unless you pick up the phone first!

Create a Company Profile and claim your logo to marry up with your personal page.

Be clear to showcase your Products and Services.

Consider it a squeeze page to your personal profile where all the real action takes place.

Again, ensuring keyword optimisation for relevant searches.

When you make updates here you need to be sure you update the details everywhere. Website, other social channels – keep a list.

Features on the Company pages include claiming hashtags, inviting colleagues and connections, promoting events.

These features are growing as LinkedIn see the value in promoting businesses.

Groups are a great place to interact with people with similar interests who you may not be connected with.

The benefit of spending time looking for good groups to join are that you can message 2nd and 3rd degree connections.

Some will only target their posts into Groups.

You may want to create a Group of your own.

Try looking for local networking groups or associations you are a member of as a starter.

I am hoping that has given you good reason to populate your LinkedIn profile.

This exercise also consolidates who you are, who you are looking to find and what value you can bring to your customers.

You must write about yourself and put time into it.

It will never be finished.

I am laughing at this myself because there is always some new ideas or information that is worth reviewing and sharing.

It is a constant work in practice but starting is better than doing nothing.

Now we need to talk about how you actually use LinkedIn to grow your network, find the right people to get more meetings and create long lasting business relationships...

It breaks down into two sections.

1. The Feed
2. Your Network

Your profile feed will show you posts from everyone you are connected to and the comments or interactions they make on their network.

It seems complicated at first, but you get used to it.

You have control over what you see in your feed.

The three dots on every post will be a lifesaver.

Use the dots to improve your feed.

Decide who to follow or not from a fresh page.

There are many reasons to spend a little time here:

Your connections may not be posting so why follow them? By unfollowing you remain connected.

There may be people following you that you want to follow back.

Your main focus on the Feed should be about participation.

Participation is key.

Use the Feed to find your ideal customers posts and share your own insights.

Remember not to be salesy or spammy.

You are sharing your views.

In the off-line world of networking there is a saying: Visibility + Credibility = Profitability.

In simple terms – the more you are visible in your contacts' minds the more likely they are to contact you or think of you for a relevant reason – which may lead to business referral, hence profitability.

Endeavour to look at your Profile Feed every day and share relevant content posts with context.

This encourages engagement with you.

Every time you update your profile and show activity – you are 'visible'.

Every time a person likes or comments or shares on a post it is pushed back into the feed.

By joining in with your connections conversations in their posts you will also be exposing yourself to their network extending your potential reach.

When you have added value in a conversation that resonates with someone else that has engaged, they may invite you to connect.

Similarly, it works the other way around for you to see who you may invite.

Targeting your content to speak to your ideal customer is the key.

Showcasing your products or service are simply not enough these days.

You really want to be sharing stories about what you have done for your customers and how you have made them feel.

Remember recommendations?

You can now copy and paste that text and craft a lovely image to share with contextual content in a post.

Articles are a longer form post that can really highlight your authority on a subject allowing you to go into much greater detail.

Which brings me quite nicely to the other key area of using LinkedIn.

Your network and how to treat them.

A personalised message is always best when inviting people to connect.

LinkedIn has a prompt for you to add a note before you hit send.

They have done this for a reason.

It is proven that people are more likely to connect with a warm well written invitation.

People appreciate the effort you make when adding personal context

For example:

Great meeting you at ABC event

Or

I would like to keep in touch with what you are up to by connecting

Or

I spotted your profile; it is really interesting and even LinkedIn keeps suggesting we connect

The jury is out amongst LinkedIn professional trainers on sending a personalised note.

The argument is that your profile should be clear, compelling, and convincing enough for that person to accept your invite.

I will let you decide...

Okay, so now you have invited them, what is next?

They accept! Hooray!

Send them a thanks for connecting message.

Use your manners.

Add an open question.

Think about it.

This is the perfect opportunity to strike up a conversation.

A simple 'how have you been?' type of message can lead to the most startling of responses.

I use this 'LinkedIn is a great platform to start new conversations.'

Ultimately, your goal will be to encourage an offline conversation in as natural fashion as possible.

Avoid the temptation to attempt to spam or directly sell with InMail messages.

People will disconnect with you faster than you can blink if they think you are just there to sell your wares.

Think about it.

When we are offline and networking face to face, we engage, we listen, and we nurture people.

We do not spam them.

If someone is specifically discussing something you have a solution for - then sure, I would encourage you to engage - but listen first - do not spam.

Relevancy is key.

I often get spammed about training - or do I want a marketing plan! Err no thanks - have they even bothered to look at my profile!

You will feel the same way, I am sure of it.

Treat people how you would want to be treated.

InMail Is also a great way to see your engagement grow through the prompts you receive in your notifications.

LinkedIn keep you up to date with your network when events affect them.

You can play the algorithm game by using these notifications to your advantage plus it is a lovely way to stay in touch with your network.

Be there changes to:

Congratulate a new role or promotion or work anniversaries

See who's celebrating their birthday

These are ways to subliminally stay front of mind by sending a:

Congratulations on your new role! You must be excited?!

Well done on earning your promotion!

Happy birthday! Are you taking the day off?!

Better still – send them a voice message!

Helping your network celebrate from these notifications work towards the LinkedIn KPI's.

Check your score here:
https://www.linkedin.com/sales/ssi

You will be scored on your Industry rank plus your Network rank against others in the same industry and based on their activity.

At the time of writing this, my own score was 81 out of 100 with top 1% in the field of Professional Training & Coaching & top 1% of my network. The LinkedIn community stood at an impressive global total of 706 million users.

When you check this out, LinkedIn have provided some great short videos to help you improve the four core areas.

They are also aimed at getting you to upgrade and pay.

I have only ever used the free version, you might note, but it is personal preference and down to your acceleration expectations that will drive that decision.

Sending lots of invitations that go unanswered do degrade your score too, so it is worth withdrawing any over a month old assuming they are not particularly active or interested.

Being targeted with who you want to connect with will make a big difference to your acceptance rates.

The beauty of LinkedIn is that the demographic information is very granular.

Using the Advanced Search feature in the People section can allow you to drill down to job title and location with three free managed saved searches.

For example:

Sales Director in United Kingdom will create a list of 910,000 results.

By drilling down the filter to 2nd degree connections only the list reduces to 318,000 results.

Therefore, the more specific and targeted you are will create a much more manageable list to begin your connection request invitations.

My personal recommendation would be to save three searches based on your most local towns and cities.

In this example I have filtered it down to 10,000 results with my three town criteria.

Should keep me busy!

The search alert can be delivered to you via an email notification to your inbox allowing you to manage your time and activity around growing your network.

Who knows how long this feature will stay free to users when they are looking to upgrade you?

Let your contacts in your phone book and on email know they can connect with you on LinkedIn.

The platform will encourage you to import your contacts and invite them all.

BUT Be Aware!

If you have a large address book you could be penalised for spamming too many people in one sitting.

Go easy with this function and be selective.

Separate your motivation into sections.

For example:

Customers first

Suppliers next

Lapsed accounts

Friends and Family...you get my drift.

If you have the details in Outlook or on a spreadsheet the best way would be to import small amounts of data by uploading a CSV file.

By being connected you will never lose that person even if they move company.

When I meet someone new and I have their business card I always send them an invitation with a nice targeted message.

Doing this means that I keep a virtual database of contacts and the message will remind me of how we met.

On the mobile version the Find Nearby feature is handy when you are at an event.

It will ping with who else is on LinkedIn in the vicinity and allow you to connect.

You need Bluetooth on for both parties for it to work but a real time saving tip.

Asking your connections for a 'get introduced' to someone outside of your network is a powerful referral process.

Offer to do this for your connections.

Group chat facility allows you to bring people together in a less formal way too.

I set up folders in my inbox to track my activity on LinkedIn.

Every time a connection is accepted or sent you will receive an email notification to your inbox (presuming you tell LinkedIn to do this, that is).

I follow this simple system and you may find it beneficial too:

LinkedIn Chats

LinkedIn Dream connections

LinkedIn New connections

LinkedIn Search Alerts

I suspect you are ahead of me in what I do with this now!

It is simple – I review the chat and dream folders to be sure I stay in contact with them.

The search alerts are filed once I have reviewed the potential suggestions.

And the new connections are filed once I have sent a thank you note.

I keep on top of my activity and my inbox.

Win – Win!

Company pages allows you to send a post to colleagues but not from the personal profile – yet!

The possibilities are endless on how LinkedIn can be used but the key is consistency.

Certainly, you can do a whole heap more when you upgrade but I cannot talk about that as I have no experience in using it.

What I do know is that the free version, to date, is plenty for me and you to start new conversations with people who we want to do business with.

LinkedIn makes regular updates and their help facility is, well what it says on the tin, a real help!

The best advice I can give any user is to follow the prompts that LinkedIn give you at every stage.

If they send a notification act on it.

The psychology behind the platform is to encourage as much engagement as possible in as human a way as you can online.

LinkedIn updates their user experience regularly. It is good advice to follow LinkedIn trainers for tips they share in the feed.

FABTECA

I first came across this acronym in a presentation led by Jane Pallister.

It describes a method of presenting information in a beneficial and composite way.

Jane has lots of ology's and a very knowledgeable lady who has given me permission to share this over the years.

I think it breaks our marketing and sales messages down into a really simple guide.

When we think about what to write in a post or what to define as the purpose of a conversation it can be difficult to pin one thing down.

We naturally want to give as much information as possible.

By sharing one point well we can better understand what our customers are looking for.

Look at these pointers and make your own notes for each of them.

Consider how this will improve your communication both online and in the real world.

- Features – an overview of what the company, product or service does

Answer it here:

- Advantages – focus on aspects of the products and services which create clear and measurable benefits

Answer it here:

- Benefits – detail on the benefits created by these products and/or services(s)

Answer it here:

- Target – who the product or service is aimed at and why they are the target (customer circumstances, market trends and potential need)

Answer it here:

- Evidence – research and independent proof that what you offer really works as promised (data, statistics, research, case studies, portfolio, client testimonials

Answer it here:

- Confidence – accreditations, skills and experience, subsidies, discounts, special offers, grants – anything that increases the customer confidence levels and reduces risk of dealing with the business for the first time

Answer it here:

- Action – an action point: email us, call us, arrange a free no-obligation consultation, presentation, or site survey

Answer it here:

BUILD YOUR EXAMPLE

Features

Advantages

Benefits

Target

Evidence

Confidence

Action

NOTES:

General Observations

You thought this book was going to be all about telemarketing, didn't you?!

Well, since WAG is my third business after two failings and learnings, this is my opportunity to set you up with some good old-fashioned advice.

It is my belief that everything I talk about here will improve your confidence, mindset and approach to having meaningful conversations on all levels.

Think about it.

6 Steps to Building a better business:

1. Mastery – be the best in your marketplace
2. Niche – offer something that makes you stand apart from the competition
3. Leverage – aim high and leave room to negotiate (it keeps the conversation going)
4. Team – nurture and develop your team to their best abilities
5. Synergy – ensure everyone works together
6. Results – strive for realistic results and reward!

5 Ways to Achieve a better business:

1. Lead generation – phone, e-shot, direct mail, advertising, referrals etc
2. Conversion – know the average amount of leads that will convert to business
3. Average Sale Value – know your customers price point
4. Average Transactions – know your customers targets
5. Profit Margins – this will lead to a realistic sales target

Treat the people in your network like a Ladder of Loyalty:

1. Suspect – do not know them from Adam
2. Prospect – you know they use what you have to offer
3. Shopper – they are ready to buy
4. Customer – they have bought from you
5. Member – they belong to your brand
6. Advocate – they will recommend you when asked
7. Raving Fan! – they will recommend you of their own free will!

Brand

A little word with big consequences.

Streamline these areas and make it watertight.

This is the equivalent to your tone of voice online and the impression you will emulate wherever you leave a mark.

1. Image
2. Logo, colour scheme and fonts
3. Words & Value
4. Consistency
5. Perception of profile
6. Website
7. Social Media

I think I have said just enough for you to find value and reflect on areas that can help improve your success.

Now let us get back to 'Making Conversations Count' shall we?!

Customer Records

In my first ever role as an account manager, I was shown how important it was to keep a track of vital information.

These details would be passed on to the salesperson attending any meeting I had arranged. I would give them a snapshot reminder of what has been discussed and the expectations they have in terms of outcome from the meeting.

It effectively managed the communication between all parties and kept an agenda to stay on track and measure how well we all acted.

Understanding how long a conversation has been going on gives an indication as to whether there are any difficult factors still to be resolved.

It also allows you to maintain a high level of customer service knowing exactly what is always happening.

The fields on the next two pages are an example of record keeping.

Some of this can be gleaned from LinkedIn profiles and pages. Research your prospects.

Take a moment to read through and consider what you need to record.

Telemarketing Data Sheet

Lead Initial Call Date:

Team member:

Date Meeting arranged:

Date Meeting to be held:

Meeting time:

Team members attending:

Company contact:

Company name:

Address:

Phone:
Mobile:
Email:
Website:

Type of business:
Employees:
Turnover:
Years trading:
Position in company:

Social Links:

Key Challenges
Time scales
Money
Team
Comments:

What other information do you need to gather?

Who else will influence any decisions?

This information can be the backbone for any CRM system you may want to start using but an excel spreadsheet will suffice.

Let's start to build your list…

Finding the right people

You now understand the importance of speaking to the right person for the right reason.

Thinking about LinkedIn as the Yellow Pages directory of the now (showing my age!) you can research and invite the right people to your network.

There must be people you know that you would love to work with.

There must be companies you already know you would love to work with.

There must be people in a company you can find that you would love to work with.

These people are going to be a great starting point. So, I am asking you to make a list of those ten we mentioned earlier.

Go back to page 44 cross check and see who you would bring across now as your top ten.

Make a new list and research them on LinkedIn, their website and Google them.

What key observation led you to decide on them?

My Top Ten New Customer List:

1. Name
   Observation

2. Name
   Observation

3. Name
   Observation

4. Name
   Observation

5. Name
   Observation

6. Name
   Observation

7. Name
   Observation

8. Name
   Observation

9. Name
   Observation

10. Name
    Observation

How did you get on with your observations?

The key here is to look for things you share. It doesn't have to be all about work.

Even better when that commonality is on a personal level.

You may feel comfortable engaging on those topics that resonate with you when they post about it.

This will build visibility and increase your chance of becoming a connection.

Lining yourself up perfectly to pick up the phone and have a conversation starter.

How to Build Rapport

Building rapport is not just about making friends with the prospective customer.

It is about building trust.

Can they trust you to solve the problem they have?

They may not feel they have a problem; your challenge is to present the solution.

Even if you are a likeable person and they find you funny, if they do not trust you, they will not do business with you.

Develop an interest in the decision maker, not just their potential business or appointment.

People can spot a mile off if all you are interested in is yourself and have a 'what's in it for me' attitude.

How do they know this?

Because they can spot those that always talk about themselves, who use words like me and I instead of we or ours.

Be polite and courteous always.

This starts from the moment you say the first words, your tone of voice and the decision maker hearing that smile.

Or when you meet them and the firm handshake of their hand whilst maintaining eye contact and looking at them during the conversation.

They say eyes are the door to the soul – I say that the eyes are the door to the sale.

There are four key personality profiles, and everyone fits into one of them, even loosely. I spoke about them earlier.

You need to learn how to deal with the four different profiles because you will deal with each personality type in its own unique way.

This is all about understanding your prospect and being on their wavelength.

This will help in the sales process and therefore give you every chance of closing that all important deal.

Set yourself a task to investigate the four different styles and which one you are.

It could be a great observation when you research their profile.

Read their posts to consider whether their personality comes through.

There is a great saying when it comes to building rapport – you have two ears and one mouth.

Be sure to do lots of listening. Or reading!

With the right questions it will be easy for the prospect to share their details.

Bible questioning words start with: Who? Where? What? When? How? Why?

Speak when it is appropriate.

Learn about the person.

You should be able to recognise when you are talking too much. This is a good time to give them back control of the conversation. Try interjecting a new probing question.

Ask lots of questions – without being annoying!

It can be a difficult balance and is best when the conversation is taking a natural path.

Refresh your questioning if you find the people you are speaking with only say yes or no instead of the anticipated reasoning behind their answer.

Encourage them to talk about themselves, their experiences, their views, and opinions.

You can even ask them their advice on a subject.

This makes you more human and approachable - not the typical salesperson that is only interested in their money or what you get out of it.

You will be amazed at the respect you will gain.

Make a note of the details they share because when you next have a conversation it may be after their family holiday.

Did they share they were planning a holiday?

The best conversation opener the next time you call will be to ask them if they had a good holiday...

Relax and think of this as a face to face meeting.

You are interviewing them.

You will be asking the questions and listening intently to their answers whilst thinking if this person is suitable for you to work together too.

When listening be sure to hear the hidden questions often disguised as a statement.

You may need to probe a little deeper.

What was it about that experience that makes you say that?

How will you be able to make sure that does not happen again?

They will be looking for reassurance whilst building trust.

Can they help you get to where you want to get to?

I mean they are genuine, not time wasting and serious about keeping in touch for all the right reasons.

We have all been to a family wedding, christening or funeral where we reminisce. We have a lovey time and promise to do it more often and well, we don't.

This is where you need to be a good judge of how to spend your time wisely and with promise.

And...Most importantly, can you really help them?

When you get to this point, get excited!

Your conversations are counting!

By doing these things, keeping it real and natural you will take the pressure and the stress out of the conversation.

You will create amazing results!

Okay so here we get to refresh what we have been talking about...well, you've done all the listening!

Build a Campaign

Gather a cleansed list of cold target prospect companies.

Identify a product/service that matches the prospects.

Produce a supporting marketing piece that can be sent in support of the call.

Positioning

You have an accurate profile to reflect the nature of your role.

You will be able to help any potential or existing connections.

Consider your branding guidelines and personalising content.

Research

All Company details should be confirmed.

Where possible check fiscal background checks on financial performance.

CTPS screening validated.

Customer website address, corporate information and social media links reviewed.

Individuals should be in a specific position of responsibility.

Are there any additional members of staff that could influence decisions?

How to get past the gatekeeper

Personally, I hate this term 'Gatekeeper'.

Whomever answers the phone when I call has a job to do, just like me.

If they have been told to keep the calls from going through it is a strong chance that they are in the middle of something big.

Do you like to be disturbed if you need your full concentration?

No, me either.

Think about it.

There is something big going on.

The person answering the phone may have a fair idea what that is.

This is a perfect opportunity to bring them onside.

When I speak to what I would call an influencer, I always ask for their help.

By asking for help they generally want to do what we all love to do.

They become helpful.

Here you can determine the best way to introduce yourself.

It does not mean you have to go full chapter and verse into what you do but you can ask two key questions:

Is XYZ still the best person to speak to that handles the XYZ?

This gives an impression you have spoken before because you have done your homework.

And

I would really like to speak to XYZ but appreciate they are busy. Would they mind if I drop them an email with more up to date details before I call again?

This will give you chance to qualify the right email format and make a good first impression into their inbox.

The chances are when you follow up, because let us face facts, that is the most realistic outcome on your very first call, they will remember you.

When that person tells who you need to speak to that you were really friendly or not too pushy, it can be a fantastic referral in.

Remember the main ways to build rapport we went through earlier?

In brief they consist of:

1. Trust
2. Be interested
3. Politeness
4. Match personality

5. Active listening
6. Open questions
7. Encourage conversation
8. Relax and be authentic – that means be YOU!

Introduction

Please can you help point me in the right direction?

Who would I need to speak to that would organise…?

OR

We have on our records XYZ as being the best person to speak to. Is that right?

OR

Does XYZ still look after sourcing XYZ?

Find the version that suits you best.

Yes or No – You have Options

Yes

Would they be free for a quick chat?

OR

No

Would they be happy to receive the details on email, since they are busy?

This should confirm you have the name of the right person who will understand what you are about to offer them.

You may only get one chance to take an email address where you can send a supporting intro before following up.

Not the right person

Ah, things do change. Who would the best person be to introduce myself to now?

Take note of the right person and ask if they are available.

You will either be put through or asking to send some information at this stage.

When you get put through, it is always a good idea to introduce yourself and in the same breath (not sentence – that would be too long) ask them to confirm they still look after the XYZ.

Following up

Step 1

Good morning / Good afternoon. Would it be ok to speak to XYZ (insert name)?

The person may not announce themselves, so this gives you a moment to judge pitch and tone and stay professional.

Step 2

Introduce yourself

Repetition of the introduction with the gatekeeper with slight modification.

We have been advised that you would be the best person to speak to regarding XYZ. Is that right?

Yes

That is great news! Move to Step 3

OR

No

Oh, I do apologise. Would you be able to pint me in the right direction please?

Always be prepared that you may not have been given 100% accurate information.

Some products and services are complicated to keep brief in an introduction and can be misinterpreted. Adjust if this happens a lot!

Step 3

Please let me explain the reason for the call today.

OR

You are probably wondering why I am calling you today.

Here is where your intelligent research plus any online engagement can seriously add value to a real-world conversation.

Well, you know how...

- I loved your post on LinkedIn about...
- When I saw your comments about XYZ I knew I had to call to introduce myself
- I called a couple of days ago and sent my details on email
- We recently connected on LinkedIn
- We met at XYZ event (add detail of date and location)
- You requested the brochure on XYZ from our website
- The recent announcement from XYZ will affect XYZ

Think about it.

Create your own openers that will be relevant to how you want to start the conversation and why you are reaching out. **Tell me about yours.**

Answer it here:

This step concentrates on building the relationship and trust.

The reasons why you should be having a conversation.

You must show that you have thought about matching your products and services to meet their business needs.

Step 4

For the conversational types:

When the customer answers their phone with enthusiasm.

Good morning / Good afternoon XYZ,

Take a breath

My name is XYZ from XYZ and I would like to introduce myself

Take a breath

But I think it would be great to understand how you currently do things when you need XYZ first.

Take a breath

This approach will let the prospect do all the talking when they respond.

They will explain their current situation and any changes they are planning.

You can even add:

I know this type of XYZ is not reviewed that often, so I do not want to take up your time if it is not a priority now.

This shows that you have common sense and appreciate their time.

It breaks down barriers when handling a sales call that you are not looking to be pushy and would rather be helpful.

The customer will be inclined to give you a brief overview of the situation and the conversation can begin.

You are now building rapport and creating a space in the future to be invited back to speak to them when the time is right.

You have all the reasons why your product or service is so great.

You have all the reasons why your customers, like them, benefit from working with you.

You have the objections and can listen and build a case around their needs.

You should agree when they say they need to be cautious of change or careful over budget.

When you can tell they are busy or not listening:

When the customer answers their phone abruptly.

Good morning / Good afternoon XYZ,

Take a breath

My name is XYZ from XYZ and I would like to introduce myself

Take a breath

Is this a good time for you?

Take a breath

When they answer no reply with:

NO. Okay, I will be brief then

Take a breath

I would like to find out more about how you currently do things when you need XYZ.

Be direct.

Allow them to respond and repeat your questioning as far as you can without overstepping the mark.

On this count you will have to be your own judge.

Your questions will come up in all different variations.

Keep a track of which ones hit the mark.

Encourage deeper responses with open questions to draw out the information you need.

Like:

'Tell me more about that.'

Or

'Let me understand your plans.'

These options should be all about the prospect and the qualifying questions you need to identify.

Examples can be:

What do you buy already?

Where do you buy it?

Why do you use them?

How does this affect things?

What are the next steps?

Who else is involved in the project?

These types of questions are designed to:

Allow you to collect more information

Give an illusion of control

You bring everyone else involved into the equation

Trust your instincts and follow the process.

Step 5

What is in it for them?

This is when you can capitalise on a solution to meet a need the customer has identified or to handle an objection that you can solve.

I just found out...

- We have announced some new product services you might be interested in that will affect your future decisions
- There have been some changes you need to bear in mind
- It has been some time since we last spoke about your plans for XYZ

At this stage, your customer should only be feeling that you have called to help.

Recap with the prospect what you have discovered and how you are able to help them.

Think about it.

What could you tell them today that will interrupt their thinking about XYZ that will put you at the front of the queue to get the business done?

What will they just find out?

Answer it here:

Next Actions

This is the Close.

It does not have to be scary.

It should not be awkward.

This beautiful step is about 'Making Conversation Count'.

When you talk to someone at length, maybe tried them numerous times and you have never given up, this is your reward for doing a great job.

You know you can help; the customer knows you can help.

The next step is for both parties to explore how they can help each other.

You are taking it to another level in relationship building.

It does not mean you have won the business – Yet!

You need to identify what the next action will be.

Do you arrange to go back when the timing is perfect, or can you move ahead now?

For customers who need face to face

Would you be happy to meet to discuss this in more detail?

Build on the fact that there is need for greater discussion.

Bring up any documentation that you may need to be able to offer the most accurate advice.

Offer to include anyone else that is vital to the project to be included.

When is the best time to meet?

Customers can have different approaches to their schedules.

I have come across those that have a set day for appointments.

There are those that prefer to meet in the mornings.

Be prepared to change your own schedule if it is the difference of the meeting going ahead sooner than later.

I have my diary here to allow me to get it booked in and I will send you a confirmation to your electronic calendar.

Showing you are organised confirms their impression you gave in the conversation.

You may use shorter sentences.

You may use excitable language and that is OK!

For customers not ready yet

Would it be ok to EMAIL you with more details and call back on [DD/MM/YY] to discuss this?

YES

Take the full information that you need if you need to quote a price.

Explain it will be guide price.

Confirm date and time you will follow up based on contract timelines or priority timescales.

Ask for the best email to send it.

NO

Let me explain why it is important to inform you.

When would be a better time?

Agree the next best time to contact them.

STILL NO

Agree with them that this is fine.

You cannot win them all!

They are not your ideal customer.

Move them to an email or direct mail campaign so you can send information via a newsletter.

Answerphone message

Hello, it's _______ from _______

It is important that we speak, my number is _______

If I don't hear from you in the next few days, I will call again.

Always leave a message when you hit an answerphone or voicemail box.

You should be able to portray you are friendly and approachable.

It allows the customer to look up your number and do a little background on you.

We do it when we get calls, don't we?!

If they try several times without a message, we immediately jump to the conclusion they are trying to sell us something.

What do we do to those callers?

Yup, we ignore them or worse still, block them.

Make them want to answer your call from the message you leave and the impression you have already made.

Remember if you are engaging with these people online already you need to reflect that image, they have of you.

Key Benefits Examples

Here are some examples of why customers will consider using you:

- Award winning business
- Proven track record
- Return of investment
- People buy from people
- Value is not always about being the cheapest
- Understand a complex problem and create a simple solution
- Experience in the industry
- Know what works
- A company you can trust
- Speak to real people
- Always striving to be the best

Think about it.

What are your key benefits?

Answer it here:

The Big Follow Up

So, you will be better able to get past the Gatekeeper.

You will be better at opening the conversation.

What will you do if you cannot get hold of them after a few attempts?

Simple.

I use the three-strike rule.

I do not count sending an introduction email.

I only count the times I have tried by phone.

On the first call you need to support it with your email.

Forewarned is forearmed.

The customer has your information and so long as they have read it (because you've written in a clear, compelling way) they will anticipate you trying to contact them again.

Be clear in your message and in your email that you will try again.

It is okay that they do not take your call.

You may be the best answer to their problem.

BUT they may not need to deal with this problem right now.

Consider the timing and move the call in your calendar forward no more than 90 days.

This is considered the longest time between getting in touch called Constant Contact.

Over time they will get to know you from your messages, emails, and any online presence so that when the time is right, they feel like they already know you.

Regardless of whether you have spoken or not, every piece of communication will play out like a conversation to your customers.

When you cannot reach someone on the phone, yet you have them in your network on LinkedIn, for example, turn the conversation you want to have into a post.

Using convincing storytelling about how you have helped a specific customer solve a specific problem will build what marketers refer to as:

Know, Like & Trust

You should be aiming to use your content marketing to speak to your potential customers online.

There are other platforms and I do not want to do a disservice to them.

As with all projects it is best not to over complicate it or leave you feeling overwhelmed.

Where you have a catalogue of great visuals that tell their

own story about how you help drop them onto Facebook or Instagram.

When you get quoted text back from customers saying how great you are that is perfect for Twitter.

Why not create a YouTube channel for your videos?

It is all about knowing what works well on the platform and who hangs out there.

Trial and error but whatever you do – stay visible!

From any post you put out there be sure to connect with people that respond.

Encourage that first conversation.

Invite people to join you not just to be part of your network to become a number.

Know your network.

Make every effort you can to get to know them and what they need.

It is not who you know.

It is not even what you know.

It IS about what you know about them that counts.

You are ready to begin ‘Making Conversations Count’.

Start with ten.

Add ten more.

Then another ten.

Think about it.

Call one person per day.

That is only twenty people a month.

But that is 240 new people a year.

With conversion rates as low as 5% you will be looking at 12 new customers in the first year.

Make 2 calls per day and that is 40 new people a month, 480 new people a year equalling 24 new customers.

You do the maths.

Let us go back to the very beginning.

How many new customers do you need?

Answer it here:

How many do you want?

Answer it here:

Two different questions between the need and want.

You should always want more than you need.

Build your diary with call backs when you cannot reach them.

Prioritise your follow ups with people you have spoken to that will be closer to being ready.

Do not be afraid to ask for a virtual coffee over video chat.

Do not be shy in asking whether they know someone who might be interested.

Build a business to be proud of.

Build a business you want to shout about from the roof tops.

Campaigns to be Proud of

I could not possibly imagine how many phone calls I have dialled in my 30+ year career.

Starting out as a Tele-Sales agent was more about ringing existing customers to fulfil an order requirement on a regularly agreed basis.

Some would require two deliveries a week and have specific times when they would pick up the phone and literally shout their orders because the canteen was so noisy in the background.

Other customers would need you every few months however you would always be expected to give everyone the same level of courtesy.

Frequency did not mean those that ordered more often paid best.

Something you learn quickly.

I had customers I would make more commission from by ringing every couple of months and have a good natter with.

They would enjoy telling me about their children, the holidays they were planning or what they did whilst away.

I would always keep them abreast of anything new.

Often it was about doing your homework.

Thinking about what they could possibly use that we stocked and making sure they got a fair price to add it to their order.

Making my customers life easier rewarded me in always overachieving targets.

When you have the measure of some 7000 products AND you understand the customer database well enough to be able to support your sales team too - you get noticed.

I can still remember product codes from 1988!!

I was singled out for national accounts on top of my existing workload.

Fantastic you might think!

It was – to a point.

The profit margin was tight.

The devil in the detail meant you could not make mistakes.

These customers had expectations on another level.

They were not interested in talking about their family.

Well, not in the early days anyway!

They scrutinised every penny and every delivery to be sure they matched.

Auditing and inventory stocks like I had never experienced before.

It did teach me an important lesson though.

These types of customers do not bring you riches.

They allow you to create a backbone of infrastructure to build fatter fee earning customers off the back of.

Name dropping can prove useful to encourage new customers to join your gang too.

Using a brand name comes at a price.

You may want the kudos of working with a well-known company but remember they will have their own expectations of you too.

Look after your customers and they will look after you.

In the early days of telemarketing we were expected to dial high numbers.

The business phone book was thrown at your desk and you were expected to make appointments by hitting it hard.

There was no marketing.

There was no script.

You simply rang and asked for a meeting.

I could not imagine what that would look like today!

My success came from working from Z at the back because no one ever got to around to them.

It was not unusual to be targeted with making 140+ dials a day.

The emphasis was on quantity. But you know as well as me, quality will always win the day.

The information available to us today means that we can all work much smarter in contacting those people we wish to work with.

There is a shift in how we approach people and I for one will endorse being human and showing our personality.

My view is that tele-marketing has always been classed as the first contact and often cold which is where the term cold call comes from.

There is room now to turn this analogy around to become a qualifying call.

Make the first call your fact find.

Clarify you have the right person's details who is responsible for the products or services you are interested in speaking to.

Cleanse your data and capture the right information for e-marketing.

Find them on LinkedIn and send a personalised invitation to connect.

Arrange that exploratory call to establish need and timing.

Once you have completed this stage you move to Telesales.

These prospects are primed and scheduled for constant contact and are your account to convert.

Regular calls to keep your business in mind and stay ahead of any changes that could affect their decision-making process.

The year 2020 has seen mass disruption in business due to Covid-19.

Priorities changed overnight.

Projects were put on hold.

Technology advanced 5 to 10 years in 6 months.

The word unprecedented featured across the globe.

Attitudes to relationships in business shifted and loyalty and support became the drivers.

Our challenge is to keep these drivers at the forefront in doing business.

My strapline is to Make Conversations Count however we need to be mindful to Make Relationships Count too.

Statistics show that only 1% of buyers are ever ‘ready now’ so our efforts are required to be sure that the other 99% are nurtured for when they are ready.

You may have heard the terms hunter, farmer, gatherer and trapper.

Google it as you will find it another interesting comparison on sales personalities.

The reason I bring it up is because there are times when you need to be a little of each of them to get the best results.

Remember we want to be building meaningful relationships so it is you that they will come to you first when they are ready to make that purchase.

Do not let them get away!

A great client and now good friend, Lisa Pedley of White Crow Studios Ltd, said of my work for their business:

"I met Wendy many years ago when I was working for a different company, and she was working in-house conducting telemarketing training. After a few years, I left to set up my own 3D design studio and had kept in touch with Wendy, so I naturally wanted to bring her on board to help set up our marketing in the company as I knew her skills would be beneficial.

Initially, as we were a brand-new company, she helped to set up our social media accounts, including my LinkedIn profile, and set up a database of clients from scratch.

Wendy used her telemarketing expertise to let people know about the company and to ultimately lead them to the website, as we are a visual company this helped to further showcase our work.

As we were setting up as a small company, we hired WAG on an outsourced, flexible basis to suit our needs as we were not able to fulfil this role through our in-house staffing.

As the company developed, so did WAG's involvement in the business development, including many ideas for advertising and promotion that myself or Phil, my business Partner, would not have thought of ourselves.

Wendy generated many ideas in a proactive way to help gain clients and she exceeded our expectations.

I would always recommend Wendy, and I have done already to various companies.

She is a very professional, proactive & motivated individual who always does everything so well in a consistent manner and never gives up. It was a no-brainer for us to outsource the use of Wendy's services and she was a great help to us."

Sums up my values towards business perfectly!

I really hope you have gleaned some nuggets by spending time with me reading this book. I also hope you have scribbled in it and made plenty of notes.

Is that it? Is that the end?

Definitely not!

I would not leave you just like that…

Especially for you, my readers, I have set up a group on Facebook where I would encourage you to join, share your experiences and stories. Ask questions. And wouldn't it be great if some networking, support and business with each other happened too?!

Here is your link:
www.facebook.com/groups/makingconversationscount bookclub/

I can't wait to see you in there and get to know you and your business better.

Finally, I want to invite you to subscribe to my podcast show.

It is called Making Conversations Count – obviously!

Business leaders are sharing their pivotal moments with me that created a turning point for them. My aim is that their stories will resonate and inspire entrepreneurs, just like you!

Guests come from all walks of life. Success is measured in many ways. Every story unique.

So, if you are an Apple listener or Spotify, this one link will take you to however you want to listen.

I hope you enjoy the show and will send me your comments, share with your friends and family and subscribe so you never miss an episode.

www.makingconversationscount.studio/podcast

If you are really stuck and need my help personally you can book my diary with this special link:

www.calendly.com/wag-associates/discovery-call-book

One final thing...

How will you celebrate your success?

Be sure to anchor all your wins with a special moment you can conjure up that winning feeling every time you need a push.

Trust me, it is scientifically proven to work!

Now, go 'make conversations count' in your lives...

Wishing you every success!

Wendy

Printed in Great Britain
by Amazon

58494089R00079